A New True

GLACIERS

By D. V. Georges

CHILDRENS PRESS ®

CHICAGO

Glacier in Jasper National Park,
Alberta, Canada

PHOTO CREDITS

Valan Photos:
© H. Flygare—2
© John Fowler—19 (bottom left)
© R. Moller—19 (bottom right)
© Bob & Ira Spring—4, 14, 16, 38 (top), 43, 44

Journalism Services:
© Mark Gamba—6

Root Resources:
© Ted Farrington—8
© W. Helfrich—19 (top)
© Lia E. Munson—25 (right)
© Kitty Kohout—26

Nawrocki Stock Photo:
© Paul Sipiera—10 (2 photos), 35, 40
© Mark Stevenson—33

EKM-Nepenthe:
© Thomas Corad—12

Tom Stack & Associates:
© Tom Bean—17, 18, 41
© Kevin Schafer—22 (2 photos)
© Jim Yuskavitch—45

Photri—20

Image Finders:
© Bob Skelly—25 (left)
© Maurice Rosalsky—28 (2 photos)
© Jermoe Wyckoff—37

Cameramann International Ltd.—38 (bottom)

Library of Congress Cataloging-in-Publication Data

Georges, D. V.
  Glaciers.

  (A New true book)
  Includes index.
  Summary: Discusses the formation of glaciers and
their broken off pieces, icebergs; the way they shape
the earth; and why scientists study them.
    1. Glaciers—Juvenile literature. 2. Icebergs—
Juvenile literature. 3. Glacial landforms—Juvenile
literature. [1. Glaciers. 2. Icebergs. 3. Glacial
landforms] I. Title.
GB2403.8.G46 1986   551.3'12   85-30884
ISBN 0-516-01281-9   AACR2

TABLE OF CONTENTS

GLACIERS

Glaciers are layers of ice and snow that move. Glaciers creep down hills and valleys. Or they crawl slowly to the sea over cold, nearly flat lands.

Glaciers are surprisingly common. In fact, they are found on every continent except Australia.

Opposite page:
The Jostedals Glacier in western Norway covers 300 miles.
It is the largest glacier on the continent of Europe.

Patagonian Icecap in Antarctica

The largest glaciers are called ice caps. Huge ice caps cover most of Greenland and Antarctica.

Even near the equator there are glaciers. But these glaciers are in the mountains, very high above sea level. If they were at a lower altitude, the glaciers would melt in the warm climate there.

Glaciers are important. They contain over three fourths of all the fresh water in the world!

Mendenhall Glacier near Juneau, Alaska

HOW GLACIERS FORM

Glaciers can form at high altitudes anywhere. They form at low altitudes near the poles. But for a glacier to form, the air must be moist.

In some parts of Antarctica, it never snows. The temperature is always below freezing. However, the air is so dry that snow cannot form.

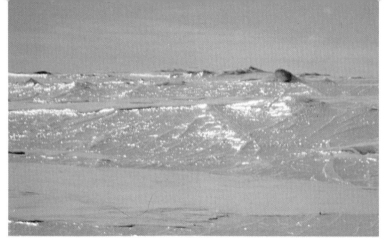

Scientists (right) must cross dangerous cracks, or crevasses, in order to study glaciers. They estimate that the ice in Antarctica's Blue Ice field (above) is one million years old.

In these places, there are no glaciers. Nothing grows or lives there, and the earth is frozen solid. The landscape is just barren.

When enough moisture is in freezing air, snow falls. In the earth's coldest regions, snow on the ground does not always melt. It gathers year after year.

When snow first falls, it is light and fluffy. Then slowly it packs down. With time, it becomes solid and slippery. It turns to ice.

We see this happen in winter, on streets and in yards.

In very cold climates, new snow falls on old ice. The old ice was once new snow, too.

Lotschenthal Glacier in Switzerland

If it stays cold, snow and ice just keep piling up. Before long, thick layers of snow and ice cover the ground.

These layers of snow and ice become glaciers when they begin to flow. The great thickness of a glacier causes it to move. The many ice layers slide past each other. The layers act like sheets of paper on a slant.

The magnificent ice caves in Paradise Glacier, Mount Rainier National Park, were formed by melting water.

As a glacier moves, its downhill part reaches warmer temperatures and begins to melt. Streams of melting water flow from under the glacier. Water also flows on the glacier's surface.

Uphill, snow may still be falling. If much snow falls, the glacier actually grows in size as it descends. Or if little snow falls, the glacier slowly shrinks.

Glaciers can be any size. In the Swiss Alps, the many scenic glaciers are a few hundred feet thick. In Antarctica, the great ice cap is over ten thousand feet thick!

Fiescher Glacier and the Walchehorn Mountain
near Grindelwald, Switzerland.

No matter what the size,
all glaciers eventually melt
or reach the sea. However,
this may take hundreds or
thousands of years to
happen.

Muir Glacier in Glacier Bay, Alaska

ICEBERGS

Does a glacier stop
when it reaches the coast?
No, it continues, flowing
out beyond the shore.
There icebergs, which are

17

Icebergs floating in Glacier Bay, Alaska

pieces broken from
glaciers, float out to sea.

Icebergs can be different
shapes and sizes. Some
are flat and thick. Others
are tall and jagged. The
largest icebergs are
several miles long.

Icebergs come in all shapes and sizes. Only a small part
of an iceberg appears above water. More than three-fourths
of it is underwater. Because of this underwater hazard,
icebergs are dangerous to ships no matter what their size.

Over four-fifths of Greenland is covered by a glacial ice cap.

Ocean currents carry icebergs far from the shore. From Greenland, icebergs travel all the way to the Grand Banks of Newfoundland. That voyage is nearly five thousand miles long.

Eventually, warm ocean currents melt icebergs. This happens just south of the Grand Banks.

In the Grand Banks, ships must be careful. Icebergs are solid and hard. They can rip steel.

In 1912, the famous ship the *Titanic* hit an iceberg. It sank quickly. Only about five hundred people survived. Three times that many died.

Polar Star, a United States Coast Guard vessel, cuts
through the ice in McMurdo Sound, Antarctica.

Today, the United States
Coast Guard patrols the
North Atlantic Ocean
looking for icebergs. The
mission is called the
International Ice Patrol.

With helicopters and
boats, the Ice Patrol keeps
track of icebergs. Ships
radio the Ice Patrol for
information. Now ships can
avoid the danger of
striking icebergs.

HOW GLACIERS SHAPE THE EARTH

Glaciers are powerful. They pull rocks right out of the earth. They leave behind a magnificent landscape.

How is this possible?

Look closely at rocks in nature. Usually, rocks have cracks. Glacial ice can seep into these cracks. Often it seeps quite deep.

Rocks (left) deposited by glaciers dot Norway's landscape. The marks on these rocks (right) in Canada's Columbia Ice Field were caused by glacial action.

Thus, glaciers do not just slide over the earth. They partly penetrate the rocks around them. Then as glaciers move, they pick up rocks and carry them along.

These huge boulders were left when their glacier melted.

Glaciers pick up all sizes of rocks. Sometimes a huge boulder will lie in the middle of a flat field. How did the boulder get there?

Probably a glacier picked it up from rocks far

away. Then the glacier carried the boulder to the field. When the glacier melted, the boulder remained.

Glaciers pluck many rocks that are side by side. The process is called gouging.

Because of gouging, valleys made by glaciers have a broad U-shape.

Clinton Canyon, South Island, New Zealand (above)
and Lauterbrunnen Valley, Switzerland (below)
are glacial valleys.

Most valleys made by streams have a V-shape. But a glacier changes the stream valley. The glacier plucks and gouges rocks from the bottom and sides of it.

Valley sides become steeper. The valley bottom becomes flatter. And the shape resembles a U.

The fjords of Norway are actually sea inlets in U-shaped glacier valleys.

Fjords are found in many other places, though, wherever glaciers gouged steep valleys near a sea.

Smaller fjords are in Alaska and Japan.

On the coast of Norway glaciers melted long ago. Then seawater crept into these tall and steep valleys. The fjords of Norway have a special beauty. They are the most famous in the world.

Geiranger Fjord, Norway

Often, different glaciers surround a single mountain. Then these glaciers pluck and gouge rocks from all sides of the mountain.

After many years, the mountaintop is sculpted into a horn, or sharp peak. This is how the Matterhorn of Switzerland was formed.

Hundreds of other horns are in the Swiss Alps. All horns are formed from the same gouging process.

The Matterhorn in Switzerland

Horns make mountains more rugged and difficult to cross. But they make the scenery quite thrilling.

With so much plucking and gouging, a glacier carries a mighty load of sediment. Big boulders and tiny grains make up the sediment. It can weigh many tons!

During melting, the sediment mixes with water. This causes it to appear dirty. From above, these

A glacial meltwater stream at Mount Rainier, Washington

meltwater streams look like
dark ribbons alongside the
white glaciers.

Sometimes the outside part of a glacier melts quickly. Then the sediment does not flow in a stream. It is deposited right next to the glacier.

Often this sediment piles many feet high. It becomes a barrier to the rest of the melting ice.

Then the meltwater cannot flow away. The melted ice just sinks into the ground. But it leaves its mark there: a big hole where the ice once was.

View of Victoria Glacier and Lake Louise in the Canadian Rockies

This hole is called a kettle. It can be very wide and deep.

Sometimes the melted ice does not drain. Then the kettle fills with meltwater. It becomes a lake.

Berg Lake and Mount Robson (above) in the Canadian
Rockies. Fox Glacier (below) in New Zealand.

WHY SCIENTISTS STUDY GLACIERS

Scientists study glaciers to find out about the world's climate.

Climates are not exactly the same every year. Next summer may be just a bit hotter than last summer. Or perhaps a bit cooler.

How fast do glaciers grow or melt? This can tell us about the world's climate.

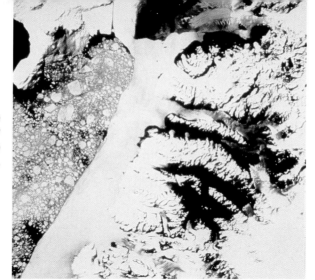

Satellite photo of the glaciers and dry valleys in McMurdo Sound, Antarctica.

From studying satellite photos, scientists tell how a glacier changes.

Satellite photos are taken over some countries every year. In other countries, satellite photos are taken every few years.

With special tools, scientists measure the size

40

Tour boat takes visitors close to the mighty glaciers in Glacier Bay, Alaska.

of glaciers from the photos. They measure both the area and the height of glaciers. Then they compare photos from different years.

Year after year, scientists keep track of the size of glaciers. They hold meetings to discuss the way glaciers change.

In fact, there is an International Commission on Snow and Ice. Over

Mount Waddington and Scimitar Glacier in British Columbia.

twenty countries belong to it. The commission meets every five years to discuss glaciers.

Winthrop Glacier on Mount Rainier is a mile wide.

Someday, scientists will discover ways to move glaciers to dry lands where their fresh water can be used. Icebergs may be towed by ship to dry areas. Or glacial meltwater

may be transported over
land in channels or pipes.
Glaciers are not only
pretty scenery. They tell us
about the climate. And
someday, they will give
fresh water to dry lands.

WORDS YOU SHOULD KNOW

altitude(AL • tih • tood)—height above sea level

boulder(BOWL • der)—a large rock

climate(KLYE • mut)—the average kind of weather at a specific place

deposit(dih • POZ • ut)—to place or drop somewhere

descend(dih • SEND)—to go in a downward direction

fjord(fee • ORD)—an inlet of the sea filling the bottom of a glacier valley

glacier(GLAY • shur)—layers of snow and ice that slowly move down hills and valleys to the sea

gouging(GOW • jing)—plucking deeply, as a glacier gouges rocks from a valley

horn(HORN)—a sharp peak atop a mountain, sculpted by glaciers

iceberg(ICE • berg)—a piece of a glacier that floats out to sea

ice cap(ICE KAP)—a large glacier, covering most of a continent

kettle(KET • il)—a big hole formed by melted glacial ice that sinks into the ground

meltwater(MELT • wawt • er)—the water that melts from glacial ice and snow

ocean current(OH • shun KUR • unt)—a stream of ocean water that is warmer or colder than the water around it

penetrate(PEN • ih • trait)—to sink into or go through

pluck(PLUHK)—to pick or pull out

satellite photos(SAT • il • ite FOHT • ohs)—photos taken from man-made satellites miles above the earth

sculpt(SKULPT)—to carve or shape something hard

sediment(SED • ih • ment)—pieces of rock, from large boulders to tiny grains, that are moved by water, air, or glaciers

INDEX

About the author

D.V. Georges is a geophysicist in Houston, Texas. Dr. Georges attended Rice University, earning a masters degree in chemistry in 1975 and a doctorate in geophysics in 1978.